Love Thos

This special alphabet book
belongs to:

_____

I love my letters!

Welcome to
Love Those Letters!

Dear Families,

Letters are at the heart of every word, words at the heart of every story. We want all of our children to be so familiar, comfortable, and confident with letters, their sounds, and the words they make, that they feel the letters *belong* to them.

You may be surprised that this book, DVD, and CD are not about teaching your children the alphabet, but about helping them fall in love with letters because they are both fun and meaningful. Helping your child fall in love with letters and words is a very important step toward your child falling in love with reading and learning.

So enjoy this book and play with letters. Say letter names and try out their sounds. Follow along on the DVD or CD and dance and sing for letters! But most of all, have fun together – not just with this set, but with the letters and words you see all around you every day!

Brigid Hubberman
Executive Director
Family Reading Partnership

Carol Cedarholm
Reading Specialist, DVD concept and co-producer
Ithaca City School District

Love Those Letters!

Family Reading
Partnership

a **Family Reading Partnership** program
with **illustrations by Katrina Morse**

A is for apple.

Are apples always red?

B is for bike.

Blue bikes are
bright and beautiful!

C is for cat.

Cats can be soft and cuddly.

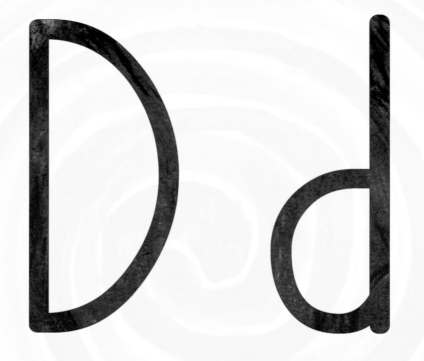

D is for dog.

Dogs like to dig in the dirt.

E is for **e**gg.

Every **e**gg cracks **e**asily.

F is for fish.

Fish swim fast and far.

G is for guitar.

Guitars make great music.

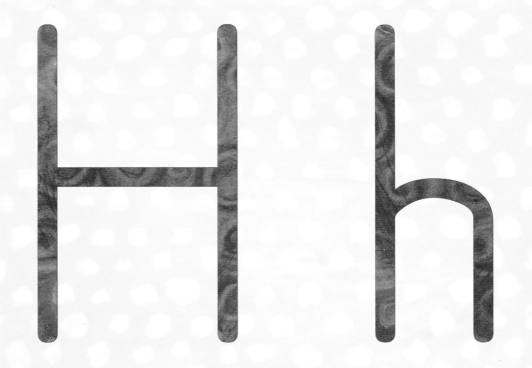

H is for heart.

Hello heart! I love you!

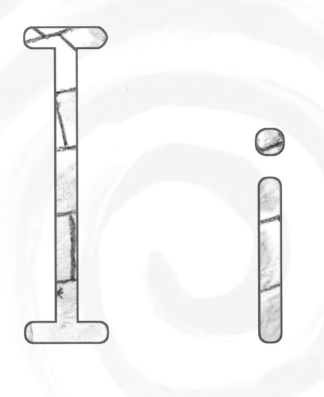

I is for igloo.

Igloos are icy cold.

J is for
jump!

Jump, jump, jump for joy!

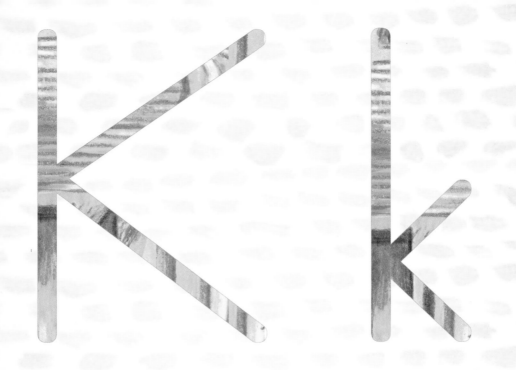

K is for key.

Keep your
key in a
safe place.

L is for leaf.

Look at the leaf flutter down to the ground.

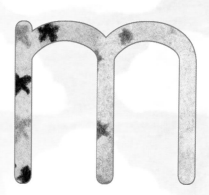

M is for moon.

Maybe we'll see the moon tonight.

N is for **n**ose.

Noses are known to sneeze now and then.

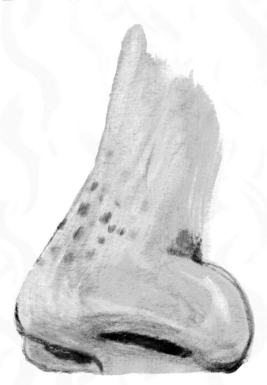

O is for octopus.

Out in the ocean an octopus swims.

P is for penguin.

Penguins
prefer to
eat fish.

Q is for queen.

Queens must be quite smart.

R is for rainbow.

Rainbows reach
across the sky.

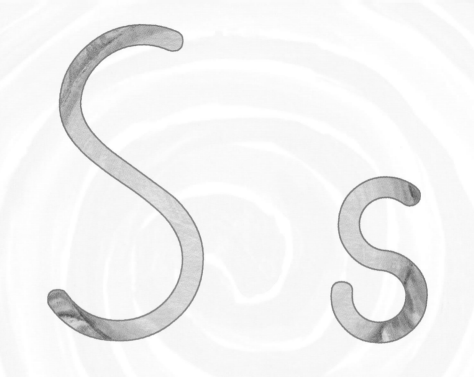

S is for sun.

Summer sun makes me smile!

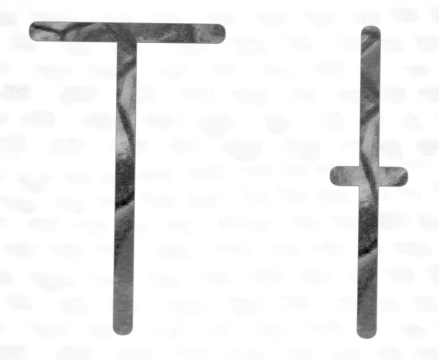

T is for turtle.

Turtles take their time.

U is for **umbrella**.

Under this **umbrella**
we stay dry.

V is for volcano.

Volcanoes erupt and lava
flows everywhere.

W is for window.

What do you see outside your window?

X is for **x**-ray.

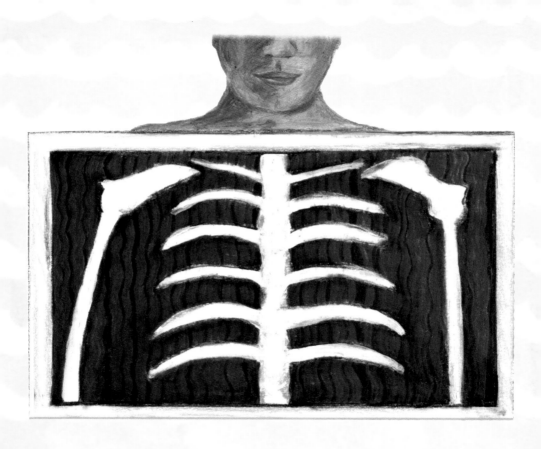

X-rays are excellent to examine bones.

Y is for yo-yo.

Yank the string and
your yo-yo will spin.

Z is for **z**ipper.

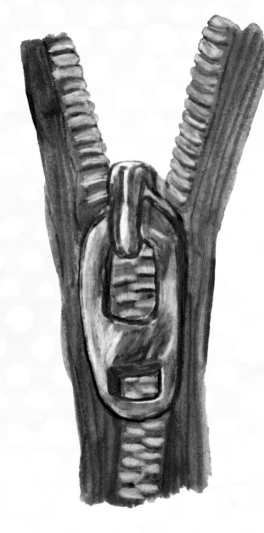

Zip up your **z**ipper to keep snug and warm.

Activities for Loving and Learning Letters!

Here are some ideas for having fun with letters, words, and stories with your child. See which activities become family favorites!

LOVE THOSE LETTERS!
Letters are made of shapes.

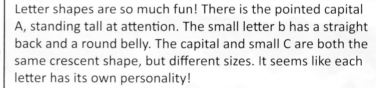

Meet the Letters

Letter shapes are so much fun! There is the pointed capital A, standing tall at attention. The small letter b has a straight back and a round belly. The capital and small C are both the same crescent shape, but different sizes. It seems like each letter has its own personality!

As you look at each letter page in the book, notice the shape of the capital letters and small letters with your child. Find things that are the same and different about the letters. Then you and your child can each trace over the letters in the book with a finger. Write letter shapes in the sand or the snow, or trace big letters with your finger on each other's back or arm.

I Spy

When your child knows a few letter shapes by sight you can play "I Spy" at home or outside. When you see a STOP sign you can say, "I spy the letter S." Once your child sees it too he can say, "I see an S on that red sign!" Now your child can spy a letter and you will have to see if you can find it. Look for letters at home on cereal boxes, magazines, and junk mail. In the community find letters on street signs, building signs, car license plates, and billboards. Letters are all around you!

Letter Art

Have your child pick a letter and draw it big on a piece of paper. Your child can color it in and add decorations. Hang the beautiful letter up on the refrigerator or a wall so your child can see it. Does your child have a favorite letter?

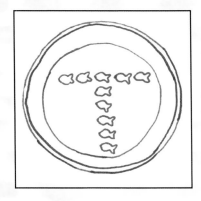

Yummy Letters

In the kitchen, you can make letters part of meals. Are you having raisins, grapes, or small crackers for a snack? Put them on your child's plate lined up in the shape of a letter. Are you putting ketchup or mustard on a sandwich? Squirt it on in the shape of a letter. Can your child guess the letter?

Letter List

As your child is learning what each letter looks like, she will also be learning the sound that each letter makes. When looking through this book, say the letter name, make its sound, and then say the word that goes with the picture.

For example, when you see the letter S, make the sound for it... SSSS, and then say the word Sssssun. What other words start with that sound? Make a list of all the words your child can think of that start with that same sound. Try it with other letters, too.

LOVE THOSE WORDS!

Words are made of letters.

Letter Cut-Out

Your child's name is certainly an important word! Write down your child's name on a piece of paper, then together look for each letter in old magazines or junk mail. Pick large letters. Cut out each letter that you find and have your child glue stick or tape the letters on paper to spell out his or her name. Hang it in a special place.

Name Poem

This is a fun word game that you can play over and over. Write your child's name down the left side of a piece of paper. Now you and your child think of a word that starts with each letter of his or her name. You can do this with names of other family members, pets, friends, or just a favorite word. Have fun!

Naming Game

Look around inside your home and together with your child, name what you see... chair, window, lamp, table, bed... and write those words down so your child can see them. Cut out the words and tape them to the objects, so your child will see the names of things he or she sees every day.

Menu Making

Write the word "Menu" at the top of a piece of paper or erasable white board. Let your child see you write the words for what you will be eating for that meal. Your child could even draw a picture of each food next to the word.

Make Lists

Show your child how words are used every day:

Involve your child in making a list of groceries, then find each item at the store. Point out the match between the word on the list and the item.

Make a list of what you plan to do together today and check each thing off as you do it.

Make a list of stories you want to read and go to the library to find each book.

LOVE THOSE STORIES!

Stories are made of words.

Love Notes

Leave a message under your child's juice glass in the morning and read it together.

Write your child's name and a note, then post it on the refrigerator. When your child finds it, read it together.

Help your child write love messages for others and put them in places where loved ones will find them later, like under mommy or daddy's pillow.

My cat went outside today.

Silly Stories
Make up a story together. Start off with an idea, like "Oliver the octopus invited some friends over to play." Ask your child, "What happens next?" From there you can make up any kind of story together, using words and imagination.

Drawing Stories
When your child draws a picture, ask him or her what the picture is about and write those words down as a caption to the drawing.

Read Aloud
Share books and stories with your child every day! Choose books that you and your child will fall in love with and want to hear over and over. Point out to your child that his or her favorite letters and words are in the story! In books you can see that letters make words and words make stories! Enjoy your time sharing books together.

Sing a Story
Use a song that you already know such as "Twinkle, Twinkle, Little Star" or "Mary Had a Little Lamb" and make up new words to go with the tune. It could be something like "Katy had a little frog, little frog, little frog. Katy had a little frog that jumped right in a puddle!" Be silly! Your child will love playing with words and making up new verses for favorite songs.

Find More Ideas and Share Yours at www.familyreading.org
Looking for more ideas? Do you have a family favorite letter, word, or story play ideas? We'd love to hear them and share with other families! Visit the *Great Ideas* page of our website: www.familyreading.org.

Love Those Letters!

© 2011 by
Family Reading Partnership

Family Reading
Partnership

Family Reading Partnership
54 Gunderman Rd., Ithaca, NY 14850 USA
www.familyreading.org

ISBN 978-0-9846414-1-3

Fonts used in this book are *Handwriting Without Tears* and *Calibri*.
Illustrations are rendered in acrylic paint with colored pencil details on hot press illustration board.

About the *Love Those Letters!* Book

This *Love Those Letters!* book was created by Family Reading Partnership as a companion to the *Love Those Letters!* DVD and CD. The colorful images and playful sentences will engage and delight children as they learn the look and sound of letters and the words they make.

Activity ideas in this book extend the fun and adventures in learning that your family can experience with letters, words, and stories as you connect the alphabet letters to real life. Have fun with the alphabet and your child will *love those letters!*

About the *Love Those Letters!* DVD and CD

The *Love Those Letters!* concept was developed by reading specialist Carol Cedarholm during a sabbatical in 2010. The foundation is a set of carefully chosen key words designed to make it easy and enjoyable for all children to learn the shape, name, and sound of each letter. Song, dance, sign language, and animation of the letters on the DVD encourage children to learn to love the alphabet and to make each letter their very own. Enjoy the song, read-aloud, and letter lessons on the CD at home or in the car.

About Family Reading Partnership

Family Reading Partnership is a national leader in community literacy efforts, promoting and supporting family, school, and community engagement around children's books and working to create a culture of literacy locally, regionally, and across the country.

For more information about our programs, and to find other products in our exclusive line of family literacy engagement tools, visit our website: www.familyreading.org.